Alexander Yuan Li

WISDOM IN COMBAT

Lion's roar of empowerment

A Theoretical Approach to Self-Defense and Personal Growth

This book focuses exclusively on the mental forces that determine victory or defeat in a self-defense situation.
The best technician will not win a fight if he lacks the mental tools.

From

Alexander Yuan Li

WISDOM IN COMBAT

Lion's roar of empowerment

A Theoretical Approach to Self-Defense and Personal Growth

Photos: iStock-525509517, iStock-1185241827, iStock-1468886187

Publisher: BoD • Books on Demand GmbH, In de Tarpen 42, 22848 Norderstedt
Printed by: Libri Plureos GmbH, Friedensallee 273, 22763 Hamburg
ISBN: 978-3-7597-7793-5

FOREWORD

A note right at the beginning:

"Fighting techniques arc not a sport and are used exclusively for self-defense! This should be clear to anyone who wants to learn them. Only in the hands of a peaceful mind do they do no harm".

In my opinion, all fighting styles are equally good and offer everything you need for self-defense. It just depends on what the individual makes of it.

"Our mental state ultimately decides whether we win or lose, not our technique."

If we ask ourselves again and again what makes the lion an excellent hunter, we come across the following attributes: Courage, patience, determination.

In order to survive a self-defense situation unscathed, we have to awaken the lion within us.

I have long considered whether it is right to write a book about the theoretical side of martial arts, as I prefer to focus on peace, humanity and mutual appreciation. However, due to social changes, I now feel compelled to pass on my knowledge of martial arts.

There are more and more aggressive contemporaries who are disturbing our peace. They are the reason why I ultimately decided to publish this book. After all, everyone should be able to defend their personal freedom.

I always publish in the hope that my book will end up in the right hands.

The following content is not about fighting techniques in detail, but about the mental tools for dealing with a self-defense situation.
It teaches us stillness, contemplation and awareness, but also concentration on the essentials. It awakens the essence of our physical abilities and makes it clear that each of us harbors a lion within us.
The reader also learns how the ego influences our lives and relationships, and how we can recognize when it has a grip on our actions.
It shows how to gain mental strength to defend your life in an emergency.

INTRODUCTION

Unfortunately, we are reading and hearing more and more about violent attacks on *supposedly* helpless people.
They often take place in broad daylight, on busy streets and pedestrian zones. Attackers proceed with extreme brutality and boldness, as they do not expect their victims to put up any resistance.
Passers-by look to the side in shame out of fear instead of intervening to help. Analyzing this passive behaviour of our fellow human beings would probably be a very interesting subject for a psychologist, but would not help us at the moment.
Let us therefore discuss how you can best protect yourself. This book is primarily aimed at women because, sad as it is, they make up the majority of victims. The aim is to help them escape the "typical victim role". But of course I am also addressing men who want to protect their family from violent attacks.
My many years of practice in various Far Eastern martial arts and the study of different human behaviors have shown me that everyone is capable of successfully defending themselves against an attacker, even if they have no experience in martial arts. Of course, this requires some techniques, but the most important point for the success of self-defense is the mental attitude.

Mental strength in particular puts you in a position to defend yourself with just a few techniques in the event of an attack.

First and foremost, be aware that every attack is extremely dangerous, which is why you *need to* acquire a high degree of discipline and willingness to act. Therefore, practise each technique regularly so that you can call it up from your subconscious with full strength and confidence in an emergency.

Discipline also includes recognizing an opportunity to escape - because the best fight is the one that doesn't take place in the first place.

Compare yourself to a warrior. They train every day for a fight that may never happen, but they are ready for it anyway. They are constantly training and trying to internalize new techniques. Of course, there are more enjoyable forms of further training. Who wouldn't prefer to immerse themselves in profound philosophical philosophical masterpieces, or embrace all people in friendship, instead of spending time studying fighting techniques.

But a world like ours, which, in addition to many beautiful things, also produces ugly by-products, forces us to develop new survival strategies.

Only those who adapt to the constantly changing situations will ultimately survive the fight. Considering how many fights you have already won in your life, learning a few self-defense techniques is just another piece in the mosaic of perfecting your personal self-defense skills.

maturation process. Think of it merely as an expansion of your repertoire of already learned movements, such as walking and standing, cycling, grasping objects, etc. Even if you have no previous experience in any kind of martial arts, this book will provide you with the necessary basic knowledge and understanding of the individual techniques and behavioral measures. But don't forget:

"Reading alone is not enough. As we all know, practice makes perfect. And fortunately, this also includes mental training, not just the sweat of physical exertion"

Only the German version is available. Please inquire about the legal situation in your own country.

§

The § 32 StGb. (Criminal Code) summarized in brief: Anyone who commits an act that is required in self-defense is not acting unlawfully.

Self-defense is a defense that is required to avert a present unlawful attack from oneself or a third party. If self-defense is viewed purely from the point of view of the law, it initially constitutes bodily harm, which is prosecuted until evidence of a genuine self-defense situation is provided.

It must therefore be clearly recognizable that you have no other choice had, than to attacker "physically" from harming you. Only if the court recognizes your actions as self-defence are you exempt from the charge o f bodily harm.

In order t o   be able to objectively assess a self-defense situation, you should bear the following in mind:

When is an attack present and unlawful? Answer: As soon as an attack on you personally, i.e. your health, your material possessions or on your sense of honor is currently being performed or is imminent.

If an attack is directed at a third party (e.g. your friend, husband, wife, child, stranger), this is referred to as emergency assistance if you intervene.

ATTENTION: Emergency assistance only exists if the attacked person is not in a position to defend himself, but indicates that he wishes to defend himself. However, if the attacked person completely refrains from defending himself, your intervention is punishable (bodily harm).
What is not so easy to understand is the necessity of self-defense, i.e. the use of the available means, taking into account the necessary dose.

This is meant symbolically:

"Don't shoot sparrows with cannons!"

The decisive factor is the dangerousness of the attacker and the conditions of the person attacked.
Experienced martial artists are required to have a special overview when using defense techniques and assessing the entire self-defense situation. However, there is no need for a warning - "Beware, I practice martial arts".
Also, in the eyes of the law, self-defense is not required if the attacked person had the opportunity to flee.
However, an escape that violates the sense of honor of the person attacked is not reasonable.

MY SYSTEM, WHICH IS NOT ONE

The pivotal point here is kicking and punching without any contact. This means that the attacker should not notice for a second that we are in defense or attack mode. Our muscles are loose and relaxed until we make contact with the opponent, whether through a punch, kick or hold. None of these techniques should be announced by an uncontrolled twitching of the shoulders, eyes or hips, and they only express their power at the last second.

Hwang, my second master, taught me to fight and I recognized in it a system which I refined more and more over the decades and made generally understandable.

Even if you might think so, there is not really a system behind it, but rather the systematic avoidance of it. Because, as in many areas of life, systems r e s t r i c t creativity. And that's exactly what my "Non" system. Everyone should learn to make maximum use of their individual abilities.

Perhaps I should emphasize at this point that, unfortunately, we also have to say goodbye to a few old, cherished myths and focus on our inner life. Only when we understand how we function can we stand our ground against an attacker.

We therefore focus exclusively on how we can defeat the opponent quickly, precisely and effectively.

At this point, I would like to make it very clear once again: my system, which is not a new martial art, merely shows how to acquire efficient mental strength. I have not reinvented the wheel, I have simply added a few training wheels.

As far as pure blocking techniques are concerned, these rarely have any significance in a street fight. To be honest, defending against a punch is a matter of luck, because it depends on how fast the attacker is and how well we react to his attack.

There are therefore only two logical conclusions.

Attack is the best form of defense - action instead of reaction!

If we don't manage to land the first blow, we have to make sure that we intercept the attacker's blow in such a way that we can

can control.

FOR THIS REASON, I ADHERE TO THE FOLLOWING PRINCIPLES:

- I stand in front with my strong foot and my strong hand.
- I breathe as smoothly and calmly as possible. I have the first stroke.
- If the opponent attacks in front of me, my strike will at least follow at the same time.

- There is no hesitation, as the situation is hopeless. I have clarified this extensively beforehand.
- If I have to distract him to create a gap for myself, I execute this distraction hard so that it has an effect. (The opponent often gives up because he realizes who he's up against).
- I did everything I could to win the battle within 3 seconds. Anything longer than this is unnecessarily risky and painful.
- I control the situation by setting the pace, force and hardness.
- When it's over, I take care of the injured person, provided I'm not in any further danger from any accomplices. Otherwise, I leave the scene and call the police and/or the emergency services.

In addition:

- If I observe that a person is being attacked, I briefly get an overview of the entire situation and intervene. Either personally or I call others for help.
- I won't give in until the victim is safe.

These are the first hurdles you need to overcome:

- Reduce the inhibition threshold.

If you want to defend yourself seriously, you cannot avoid this question:

"Am I even mentally capable of beating someone else?"
Most of my training participants only really made progress once they had learned to overcome their inhibitions. (The inhibition threshold   to physical
                        physical confrontation is higher for women than for men)

- Assess the situation correctly.

"Do I know when a fight is inevitable?"

- 100% knowledge, 10% application

"Do I realize that I have to learn a lot of techniques in order to be able to use my personal 3 - 4 punches, kicks and levers perfectly?"

- Internalize the principle of self-defense.

"Am I prepared to use my knowledge solely for self-defense?"

- See through the attacker

"Am I able to control or change my feelings, my fear and my contexts about a possible aggressor?"

- Mental readiness

"Am I ready to understand complex psychological behavior patterns?"

Explanation of the above points:

1. Reducing the inhibition threshold

I have gained the following insights from my self-defense training sessions with both male and female participants:

At the beginning of a course, almost all participants had a problem with beating someone else.
At the end of a course, everyone was aware that they had an inhibition threshold (self-awareness). 80% were able to overcome this, 19% were undecided, and 1% had even taken pleasure in hurting an attacker. (I have blocked the latter from further courses, as this group of people do not have the necessary ethical prerequisites).

Since I have no influence on who reads my book, I must now assume that you belong to the 99%.

The best way to overcome your inhibitions is to

- Sandbag training
- Pratzentraining (boxing on a punching pad)
- Breakage tests (start with simple objects where the risk of injury is low)
- Partner exercises
- Visualization of a self-defence situation through conscious emotional hygiene: perception of fear. Transforming fear into courageous thoughts (not blue-eyed arrogance, mind you)

Possible affirmations to overcome the inhibition threshold:

"I act and take the lead".
"I defend myself with all my strength"

2. Assess the situation correctly.

As already mentioned, it is best to avoid a fight. Escape should always be your first choice. De-escalation is paramount.
In order to assess the situation and the opponent correctly, you should find out the reason for the attack.

- Is it of a financial nature? Does the perpetrator want your money, your car or other valuables?
- Is it a sexual assault?
- Is it about revenge?
- Does the attacker want to boost his ego? Etc.

For whatever reason, make sure you maintain eye contact. The more often you practise this during training, the wider your field of vision will be.

Possible affirmation:

"My opponent may be strong, but I won't take any shit from him".

Questions for self-monitoring:

Am I breathing correctly? Make sure your breath is flowing. Consciously breathe in through your nose and out through your mouth.

Are my shoulders loose? Breathing properly helps here too. Am I standing in such a way that I can strike immediately with my strong foot or hand without having to shift my weight? The weight is on the back leg, the strong hand and foot are in front.

Where does the opponent offer me gaps? Check their weak points, decide on your attack strategy and act accordingly. Don't be a hero, be a pragmatist.

3. 100% knowledge, 10% application

Practice all your techniques until you have mastered them in your sleep. Then remove 90% from your repertoire and concentrate on this essence.

4. Internalize the principle of self-defense.

Only when there is no way out do we fight. But then properly, without hesitation.

Basically, I hate the thought of fighting and you probably feel the same way. But still, sometimes we have no other choice. Perhaps you can take some comfort from this.
But what will certainly reassure you is the fact that you will almost certainly not have to fight once you have escaped the typical victim role. If you radiate determination with your whole being, a suspected perpetrator will immediately sense that it would be wise to get out of your way. However, you need to practise so that you can do this in an emergency.

5. See through the attacker

Always remember: he only boils with water too.
Take a quick inventory by looking at his stature. Is he tall, strong, lanky, light, heavy, stocky, etc.? Then look in his eyes: is his gaze cold, vengeful, brutal, gentle, insecure, fearful, etc.?

Does he have weapons? If so, which ones and how does he hold them? How can you disarm him?

The latter has top priority and definitely does not tolerate any hesitation. Once again, run away if possible. If escape is impossible, you must injure him in such a way that he can no longer use his weapons against you.

6.   Mental readiness

At this point at the latest, you have to get over yourself, whether you want to or not. Muster up all your courage and don't let your emotions show under any circumstances. Believe me, fear is completely normal in this situation, but don't let it control you. They are not your fear, you are just feeling anxious. That is a big difference.

MENTAL INVENTORY

- I'm afraid of a self-defense situation!

- The subconscious and how it works

- Rules of conduct

In a self-defense situation, the pulse rate increases in all people.

The body releases large amounts of adrenaline, which can make you weak at thc knees,

Sweat appears on his forehead and his voice fails.

Adrenaline triggers fear when unexpected, sudden dangers arise. Well, fear is nothing negative at first. On the contrary, fear makes us ready to react intuitively in certain situations, to exercise caution, to flee or to fight - simply to survive.

The muscles and all the senses are then stretched to the limit. Pain is no longer perceived as strongly - we are ready to fight.

This endogenous alarm system enables us to recognize risks and influence our behaviour accordingly.

Even if we are aware that anxiety is a product of our fantastic creation and in no way harms us, we tend to regard the symptoms that occur in the moment of anxiety as a physical failure, as a gift from God.

Of course it is unpleasant to be gripped by paralyzing fear in a moment of danger. However, the real reason for this "feeling of powerlessness" has a clear origin.

A lack of knowledge in dealing with situations such as self-defense really blocks us and takes away our energy to act. Unfortunately, I am not in a position to remove this kind of powerlessness at the push of a button, but I can give you practical tips on how to achieve a more self-confident demeanor, which alone will allow you to escape the typical "victim role" or enable you to defend yourself effectively in an unavoidable emergency.

Of course, this requires your cooperation and the willingness to open up to a new, perhaps completely unknown way of thinking.

Back to fear. We are actually only ever afraid when we are faced with unexpected, unfamiliar situations.

I still remember my childhood when my father sent me down to the cellar to get him a bottle of beer.

The dark, terrifying cellar, home to countless demons, made my blood run cold.

Slowly, I descended into the world of horror. My body trembled, my legs became weak and my heart beat wildly in my slender chest.

All my senses were on edge. As soon as I saw the crate of beer, I grabbed the first bottle I could and ran back upstairs as fast as I could. I was saved.

Of course, this was not the last "cellar experience" in which I became acquainted with fear. But at some point I learned that no danger awaited me in the cellar and the fear was banished.

Of course, this is not to say that this experience can be compared with an attack on the street, although there are certainly some parallels that will be explained in the following pages.

Take, for example, the toddler who is unable to walk a few steps without help from his mother.

It is only by her protective hand that it is prepared to take the risk of running.

As soon as the mother lets go, the child becomes frightened, loses its balance and falls to the floor, which then enables the child to move forward safely and calmly using the familiar crawling method.

When you walk, do you still think about how walking actually works and what efforts and fears you had to overcome to learn it?

Probably not, right?

Although it can be life-threatening to cross a road on foot these days.

But despite the traffic density and hectic pace in our cities, we move around safely and confidently.

And this is only because we alone are able to protect ourselves from traffic and know that our learned technique of walking upright works without thinking about it.

But if you were asked to fly to the moon in a rocket today, your lack of knowledge about space travel would immediately make you break out in a cold sweat.

Every new task evokes an unpleasant feeling in us, which can actually escalate into panic.

"When we leave our comfort zone, we enter the learning zone with shaky legs. Once we have learned enough, this becomes a growth zone, until at some point it becomes a comfort zone again.

In the event of an attack on our person, we go through this cycle within a few seconds.

If you learn self-defense techniques in the same way that a baby learns to hold its bottle, you will naturally expand your repertoire of movements and strengthen your confidence so that what you have learned will instinctively come to your aid in dangerous situations. How to internalize these techniques correctly and anchor them indelibly in your subconscious will be covered a little later.

First of all, you should free yourself from the idea that a physically weaker person has no chance against a stronger attacker.

Because true power comes from the spirit. And a woman, a child or an elderly person, for example, is in no way disadvantaged.

When it comes to women in particular, I often had to watch parents influencing their daughters at school: "Stop fighting with the boys. They're superior to you in terms of strength. Play with your dolls instead, like a proper girl should!"

Just like: "Women and soccer? That's an absurdity!" But here, too, the ladies have long since proven that they are very capable of mastering this "man's game", even if women's soccer has by no means found the acceptance it deserves.

Even in a male domain such as kick-boxing, women are achieving considerable success.

If we now look at the "playing field of the street", we see that it is all too easy for women to fall back into the role of victim. The cliché of the "weaker sex" is so widespread that even those affected accept it as seemingly unalterable.

Why a man chooses a woman as a victim, whether out of uncontrolled urges or to empower himself with her handbag, we will leave aside.

The fact that women are attacked on a daily basis should be reason enough to provide you with the necessary tools for successful self-defense. However, before we begin to internalize the defence techniques, we need to create a mental basis that will enable you to act and react correctly in an emergency. To do this, it is necessary to redesign all previous mental programming.

A few examples may look like this: Old

program

- I'm scared! I can't!
- A woman is weaker than a man! You are powerless against an attack!
- I am nervous!
- etc.

New program

- I don't put up with anything!
- I can be tough in an emergency!
- A man may be strong, but I have the will and the strength to fight back!
- I know that my inner strength is helping me! I am becoming more relaxed every day!

You see, all negative thoughts can be replaced by positive ones. This does not mean that unpleasant things are simply suppressed by looking at everything through rose-colored glasses. A positive mindset is more likely to help us overcome any problems that arise instead of running away from them despondently. The purpose of reprogramming is to replace discouraging, destructive thoughts with uplifting ones.

How could a boxer get into the ring if he is convinced before the fight that he will lose?

Of course, it is not possible to change long-standing thinking overnight, but it is a crucial part of the task to be solved.

The best technology will fail if we are not convinced of its effect.

and we lack the certainty of being able to use them in an emergency.

You are unlikely to find an answer here on a rational level.

Only a constantly maturing process of rethinking, with the knowledge of how your subconscious mind works, will give you the self-confidence you need to overcome any hurdles.

PHILOSOPHICAL MIND GAMES FOR
INNER PEACE

To achieve inner peace, it can be helpful to try to look
at the world from a neutral perspective. To do this, you
first need to ask yourself certain questions and let the
answers sink in. For example:

Is there good and evil?
If so, what percentage of them do we consider good
and what percentage evil?
As soon as we try to attribute the majority to one of
the two, we leave   we   our   neutral
position. We then hold an opinion that we assume to
be true, thereby promoting either good or evil.

But what is actually good and what is evil?
As individuals, we will probably never be able to see
through the "plan" of the world/creation. Wouldn't it
be wiser to say:

"I recognize that there are both, and that I too have all
aspects
c a r r y within me?" Everyone has the choice to do
what they think is right.
do.

Is it important to have an opinion?
First of all, we need to ask ourselves what the term
opinion actually means. Basically

Only those who know nothing for certain need an opinion. Because objective facts do not need an opinion. The opposite of an opinion is knowledge. Conversely, this means that when I express an opinion, I openly show that I am merely conjecturing, i.e. arguing on the level of suspicion.

My counter-questions are therefore: Why should it be important to have an opinion? Who would it serve?

Aren't opinions the cause of conflict, discomfort and war in the first place? Holding an opinion makes just as much sense as arguing about whether the petal of the rose is green or blue.

So what could be more important than having an opinion?

The ability to feel empathy, hope and love!

Opinions give rise to morals, dogma and war.
Empathy, hope and love give rise to ethics,
understanding and peace.

Is it then right to be involved in martial arts at all? Shouldn't you rather spend your time planting trees and caring for disadvantaged people?

If you recognize the laws of evolution as an incontrovertible truth, you can see everything, such as good and evil, right and wrong, success and failure, as the results of previous actions without blaming anyone for them.

to assign. The second step is to stop looking for someone to blame and instead take responsibility for these results.

If we assume that it is in the spirit of evolution if we protect our own lives and those of our fellow human beings in an emergency, fighting techniques can also be seen in the context of love.

By learning a martial art, we also get to know ourselves. And if we know who we are and what value we have, we can also treat others with respect.

WHY IS THE EGO OUR GREATEST ENEMY?

"Because the ego is not aware of its existence! And we believe we are this ego!"

For most people, the ego is equated with the "I", which gives rise to the misperception that "I am my ego". They don't realize that the ego is just another unconscious part of their unconscious. When we allow our ego to take charge of our lives, it usually ends in a fiasco. No matter what life situation we find ourselves in, sooner or later everything will end in a fight.

This is because the ego is there to protect our body, to protect it from harm. And yet it also exposes it to the greatest dangers.

Actually, the ego should be classified as mentally ill, because that is indeed what it is.

It is particularly active in men, and since men have much greater muscular strength than women, this makes them dangerous companions.

But the ego is also the master of comparison and the prompter of provocative and inflammatory slogans:

"You're a coward" "You're a wimp" "The other person is much stronger, smarter, faster than you". The ego heats up tempers and wants to keep them apart at all costs. "You're either my friend or my enemy".

It only knows black or white, no other shades. Hate or love, death or life. The ego also hates mediocrity. It wants to win, come hell or high water. And if it doesn't win, it seeks revenge. It feels hurt, humiliated, weak, mocked, small, stupid, inferior, superior, unbeatable, immortal. But it can also make others think this way about you. An ego knows no friends, but is perfectly capable of feigning friendship. At least until it has defeated the other. When two egos fight with each other, there is no salvation. Therefore, in a self-defense situation, first check whether an ego is active, in whatever form. Either your own or that of your opponent. To recognize the ego in its full depth and to understand how it works, however, requires more knowledge, and explaining this would go beyond the scope of this book. I will therefore limit myself to a few simple, easy-to-understand examples. If you really want to get to know yourself, you cannot avoid this topic. Read books that deal with it and

Grow from the knowledge you gain in the process.

In short, answering the following questions is the best way to get to the bottom of your ego.

Question 1: Do I not only feel threatened by this person, but also humiliated?

Your answer 1: Yes

Explanation 1: The situation is serious and your ego is obviously involved. Why else could it succeed in humiliating you? Your true self is untouchable and cannot be judged, categorized, humiliated or anything else by anyone in the world.

Question 2: Am I afraid of embarrassing myself if I am clumsy in the upcoming fight?
Your answer 2: Yes, in a way.

Explanation 2: Your ego is also at play here. Realize that it's not about perfection now, but about survival. Beautiful fights only exist in the movies. On the road, the only thing that counts is saving your life.

Now let's start working on your mobility with some simple exercises.

Even if you might have sore muscles tomorrow and your tendons seem to have become even shorter, stay on the ball.

Physical fitness and mental balance guarantee a self-confident appearance and, as you already know, are the solid foundation for a good public image.and
and therefore   successful self-assertion.

FUNCTIONING OF THE SUBCONSCIOUS

Unfortunately, the subconscious became less and less important in the age of industrialization, but its role in people's actions and reactions increased considerably.

The man   became a   part   of thesociety and simply had to function as a small cog in a huge machine. With the rapid development of technology, he was simply forced to keep up. The hectic pace, stress and pressure to succeed demanded and still demand their toll today. No wonder that the "human miracle" generates billions in sales for the pharmaceutical industry every year and destroys vast quantities of alcohol.

Recognizing this process, let alone leaving it, is of course not easy.

After it was recognized a few years ago that this entire development had considerable health damage, however, people returned to old, traditional methods of healing. Homeopathy, autogenic training, meditation and yoga experienced a real renaissance, even though conventional doctors continued to treat the symptoms of stress with pharmaceuticals.

You are sure to find customers in the future who will take the easy way out, namely by taking antidepressants and tranquillizers.

Despite everything, people from the middle and upper social classes are increasingly being seen in fitness studios and yoga classes. Unfortunately, this trend - towards health through a natural lifestyle - is not as pronounced in the lower social classes.

However, I prefer to leave it to the psychologists to explain why this is the case.

From my experience as a trainer, however, I can confirm that everyone is capable of activating their subconscious, i.e. their primal power, even - or especially - in the field of self-defense, regardless of age, body type, gender or education.

The subconscious can be compared to a large archive in which all the information that affects you in the course of your life is registered neutrally. It does not differentiate between good and bad, negative or positive.

The subconscious doesn't care what we think. The stored data occasionally has an effect on our mind, which performs a certain mediating function between our subconscious and our conscious sphere of perception.

For example, sad experiences, such as the death of a family member, are consciously relived even years later.

Frightening situations that happened a long time ago come to light again.

We remember events most intensely when they are underpinned by particularly strong emotions.

As the subconscious itself does not evaluate our thoughts, we can consciously influence the "quality" of the impressions to be stored by means of emotional information. So people really are what they think.

If our thoughts are predominantly positive, we are in a friendly dialog with our subconscious.

If there are 49% negative thoughts and experiences in the subconscious and 51% positive ones, the positive part predominates. As a result, good feelings flow back from the subconscious into the conscious experience. As a result, you feel good and balanced. You therefore have the choice as to whether you forward your thoughts with positive or negative impulses to your archive for filing.

Of course, there is little we can do about strokes of fate, but we can always find two sides to our daily impressions. This depends on the basic attitude of each individual.

I'm sure you've heard what I'm about to recommend many times before, but I don't want to miss the opportunity to repeat it.

For fun, program your subconscious for a few weeks as soon as you wake up in the following way:

- Today is a beautiful day (even if it is raining)

A quote from Karl Valentin fits here:

"I'm happy when it rains. Because if I'm not happy, it rains too".

- I am able to imagine my ideal life in my mind.
- I'm looking forward to meeting my colleagues (even if you haven't liked one or two of them yet)
- I'm feeling better day by day
- I am healthy and full of life

Don't talk about your inner dialog with anyone. Try to stay out of negative gossip at work.

You will soon notice that your mood, your whole being and your relationships with other people improve.

Positive thoughts can only be enhanced by underpinning them with real feelings. The best way to achieve this is through atmospheric images that you form in your mind's eye and enjoy in the same way as if they were reality.

Experience has shown that these images are the most fertile food for the subconscious. This also requires some practice. I often hear this suggestion:

"I can't do that. I can't concentrate".
Please do not accept this NO. You can do anything if you really want it and firmly believe you can achieve it.
Take yourself to a beautiful place of your choice (in the initial phase of reprogramming, preferably before you fall asleep). Perhaps on a beautiful beach with powerful surf or on a mountain peak in soothing peace and fresh air. Put all your feelings into it. Enjoy the moment.
Smell your surroundings. Feel the ground on which you are standing, lying or sitting. Feel the pleasant warmth of the sun as it touches your skin, etc.
Your mind will relax and let you fall into a relaxed, comfortable state and restful sleep.
If you find it difficult to create such atmospheric images at first, try using simple objects, e.g. a table, a chair, an apple or a banana.

But now back to the topic of self-defense. It is precisely this type of image forming, including real films,   can be used when practicing the individual techniques.

Close your eyes and feel an imaginary attacker right in front of you.

Use exactly the techniques that are suitable for the attack you have in mind.

Your subconscious will now use this information, i. h. Save movement sequences (only with frequent repetition).

There are many martial artists who are capable of true acrobatic feats thanks to years of physical training, but who are unable to use the techniques they have learned in an emergency because they lack the necessary imagination or self-confidence due to a lack of mental foundation.

To create this absolutely necessary mental basis, you should incorporate as many feelings as possible into your training.

Whether you are fighting against an imaginary opponent or practicing with a real training partner, underpin every single movement with a strong sense of calm and security.

Even if the techniques initially require a certain amount of concentration and stamina, remain calm and persistent.

The subconscious mind then not only records your movements, but also your well-being and self-confidence.

This is the only way to turn a rational technique into an emotionally supported structure that can be recalled in exactly the same way as soon as you need it in a self-defense situation.

You will then act quickly and prudently, as you will have "reprogrammed" your fear into courage and your helplessness into self-confidence. Believe

You to your inner strength! And above all, don't put yourself under pressure!

Be happy about even small progress! Read books on self-improvement! Go in search of your true self every day.

RULES OF CONDUCT

"We don't show our fear, no matter how much we are shaking inside".

To avoid being considered a "victim" in the first place, acquire a self-confident demeanor if you have not already done so.

Concentrate fully on your breath. Let it flow calmly, do not hold your breath, do not press. Practice this at the beginning, no matter where you are walking or standing.

Look the people you meet every day in the eye in a friendly and open manner. This makes it clear that you are aware of your strength. This attitude puts you in a good position to never be treated as a victim, whether at work or on the street. Unconsciously, we all respect self-confident people far more than those who only ever see themselves as the will-less plaything of the powers that be.

- Provoke you the potential attackers/offenders. This can be done by adopting an overly aggressive attitude but also by displaying material possessions.
- Avoid secluded places such as parks, side streets, underground garages, etc. as far as possible.
- Stay in places where there are people.
- Seek the protection of the group.
- Being loud is half the battle!

If an attack on your person nevertheless occurs, act with courage.
An attacker/offender is usually concerned about safety himself. On the one hand, he is not keen to take a beating himself, and on the other, he does not want to be caught by the police.

You should therefore shout loudly for help if you are attacked. This does not mean that you should stand there motionless, but that you should actively use self-defense techniques.
If passers-by are in the immediate vicinity, speak to them directly and ask them to help you. It is often possible to persuade one or two people to lend a helping hand.
Once again, it is important to look the attacker in the eye with confidence.
If he threatens you with a weapon, give him the valuables he demands.
If he makes it clear that he i s not interested in material things, wait for a favorable

opportunity to disarm him with the appropriate techniques.
Always act with full force. You have to hurt him so that he lets go of you!

Remember that there is probably only one chance.
The best way to escape a physical confrontation is still to run away. So if you have the opportunity, run for your life.

Never play the hero!

Talk to people who practise martial arts. Take advantage of their experience. Over time, you will develop a sense of impending danger and can therefore avoid it in good time.

PHYSICAL REQUIREMENTS

Basically, it doesn't matter whether you have the agility of an acrobat or the grace of a lumberjack when it comes to self defense.
Of course, it is also a question of age to what extent you are willing or able to take on this form of physical exercise.
The fact is, however, that we cannot avoid a certain level of fitness. Don't worry, there are gentle measures to raise your fitness level to an individual optimum without putting too much strain on your joints and spine.
Swimming and cycling are probably disciplines that can be mentioned here without further ado.

Remark:

However, for your own safety, you should consult a doctor before starting a training phase to identify any health problems that may prohibit you from exercising.
Even if you don't need to be in above-average physical condition to perform the defense techniques, it has a positive effect on your body and mind. You will soon feel freer and happier.
This feeling alone gives your appearance that certain something and boosts your self-esteem. Army soldiers have to train every day to prepare their bodies for the so-called "Day X".

So that the commanders can be sure that the warriors
are actually   warriors are actually in good condition,
PTs = physical fitness tests are carried out regularly. If
a soldier does not meet the requirements, he is ordered
to do more. Unfortunately (or thank heavens) nobody
checks the fitness of us civilians.

So when did we train too much or too little?
Under no circumstances should you make the mistake
of measuring yourself against others. Every person
has different requirements that cannot be transferred.
So listen to your inner voice. Your conscience is the
most honest advisor here. But be careful, excessive
ambition is often the cause of a threatening
breakdown.
Yes, a conscience that has been silenced for a long
time is also capable of this.
Cakes, sweets, other pleasurable things in daily life
and, to put it bluntly, laziness, unfortunately too often
lead us to shamefully spurn our faithful advisor
(conscience).
Thoughts of exercise are suppressed for a long period
of time. However, as the conscience is very wise, it
waits for an opportunity to take appropriate revenge.
Unexpectedly, with a cursory glance in the mirror,
which reflects a fold in the stomach or a growing
double chin, ES suddenly goes on the offensive.
Insane training fervor breaks loose. We would like to
apologize for our unbridled lifestyle and plunge
headlong into the colourful world of sport.

Just for the intention of doing something for our bodies again,
we immediately reward ourselves with new, expensive training clothes, which usually hang unused in the wardrobe after the pre-programmed collapse or after the first serious muscle ache.

We quickly fall back into the old rut.
But it doesn't have to come to that. Communicate with your conscience every day.
Allow yourself a slice of cream cake from time to time, but then make sure you take the digestive walk your conscience demands.
First of all, it doesn't matter how much you do, but rather that you do something knowing what for.

Turn MUST into WANT!

It doesn't have to be a marathon. It all starts with the first step. As soon as you have taken this step with joy, the next one follows with enthusiasm. You alone decide what happens next.
I can guarantee you one thing: as soon as you feel like performing, you can't wait to increase the effort at a leisurely pace.
The fulfillment of this desire will be your recognition, your praise. And this has nothing to do with self-praise, which, as the saying goes, "stinks", but should rather be seen as an uplifting reward for the work you have done on yourself.

For   your   professional   activities   are
You are paid monthly. But if you are waiting for external praise for your sporting achievements, you may be waiting in vain. Nothing is more uplifting than "genuine praise". And you are the only person who is most honest with you (at least that's how it should be).

So, disregard all negative voices and concentrate exclusively on your well-being.

Swim 100m today and then go to the changing room exhausted. Don't think of any thoroughbred athletes who are not even really warm after this distance, but give yourself deep appreciation for this achievement and decide to cover 110m next time.

This gentle technique, also known as the "technique of small steps", will equip you for a healthy and happy future, whether in your sporting, professional or private life.

This will also provide you with a basis for the upcoming self-defense training.

At every course I am almost admiringly asked about my "supposed" good flexibility (I have not yet reached my personal goal, but I also use the technique of small steps every day).

I often get the impression that some course participants (men and women), when realizing their own clumsiness give up before you have even taken the first step.

But at the end of each course, these skeptics in particular are pleased to see that their efforts have not been in vain. The level of success depends of course on the individual basic requirements and personal effort.

My wish is to show that everyone is capable of increasing their personal performance and feeling really good in the process.

When we feel good, it is a sure sign that we have created harmony between body and mind. Simply visit a sports school and admit openly and honestly that you are not currently in top form. The mostly well-trained trainers will be happy to help you get over the initial initial difficulties.

Don't overdo it and allow yourself breaks, but make sure you force yourself to keep going. It's not a bad thing to have a "lazy phase", but it is a hindrance to stay in it.

VITAL POINTS - THIS IS WHERE IT HURTS THE MOST!

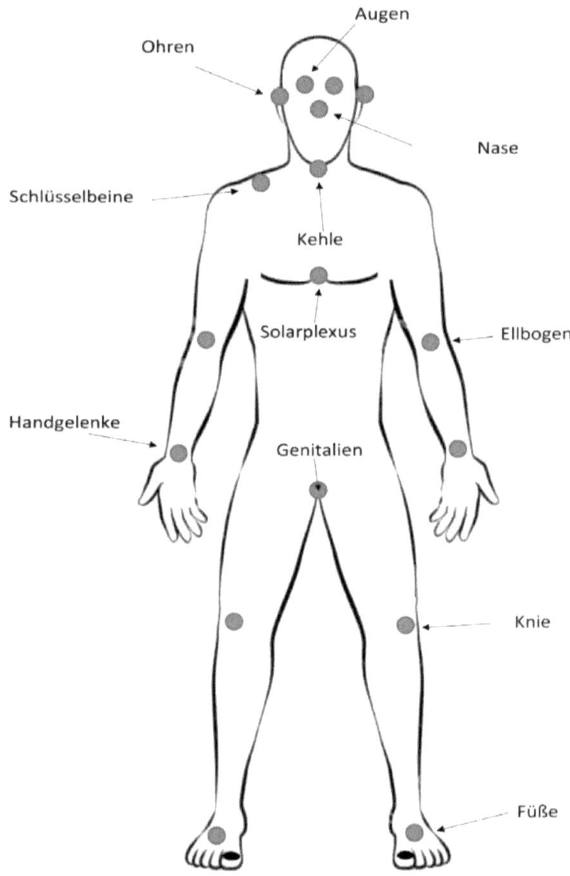

There are countless points on the human body that are very sensitive to pain, and these are often vital points.
As the word "vital" (Latin) suggests, these are vital points which, when hit, prevent an attacker from continuing his planned attack.

However, most of these points are difficult to achieve.
For this reason, I would like to show you only those that are also suitable for inexperienced people.

As you have seen from the defense techniques shown, there are a variety of possible punches and kicks to different parts of the body. Reaching these points naturally depends on the agility and skill of the respective user and on the usually different self-defense situation.
You should therefore not insist on using the knee for the injurious finishing technique after releasing from a grappling hold. A fist strike to the nose may be more effective and easier to execute in this case.
Therefore, be creative and constructive when practicing. Always perform the respective release technique correctly (as described), but recognize the best target for the final technique.
If the knee is used at the end of a defense technique shown, but you are unable to

would be easier to counter with your fist, use your fist.
Start finding your own style right from the start.

What you find easy is easier to memorize.
For this reason, I do not use fixed methods that may
not be effective in an emergency. What you   will
                              will certainly help you,
                        is   a   description of
the vital points and their possible injuries in the event
of a hit.

Try to target the individual points when practicing.
You will soon become more familiar with the
techniques and be able to use them safely and
confidently.
Knowledge of the consequences of such a hit is also
crucial for the correct assessment of a possible
deployment. After all, as we said at the beginning, we
must not shoot sparrows with cannons.

EYES

The eyes are particularly sensitive to pain and easily
injured. A targeted strike, executed with a certain
amount of force, can quickly cause the opponent to
lose his eyesight.
Please consider the issue of the "necessity" of self-
defense. Before you resort to this technique, you should
get a clear picture of the necessity of its use.

EARS

A strong pull on the ears can cause the attacker to release his grip.
A blow to the auricle is also a good way to disable your opponent. This leads to a temporary loss of orientation, but can also damage the eardrum under certain circumstances.
Make sure that your fingers are close together and your hands are formed into a hollow when performing this type of strike. The resulting air cushion increases the effect.

NOSE

The nose is an easy target. A blow with the fist or the ball of the hand is very painful, usually brings tears to the attacker's eyes and impairs his vision.

It can lead to a fracture of the nasal bone. However,

this depends very much on the force of the blow.

KEHLE

A blow to the larynx literally takes the attacker's breath away. This blow can also be fatal if the cartilage of the larynx is crushed. This injury leads to death by asphyxiation. THEREFORE, handle with care.

HALS

The blood supply to the brain is interrupted for a moment by a strong squeeze or a blow to the neck.
The opponent is dazed or partially unconscious, without life-threatening consequences.
The best way to hit the outside of the neck is with the edge of the hand.

KEYBOARD

The collarbone is also an easy target to reach and is easy to break due to its low strength. The opponent is immediately incapacitated and by no means dangerously injured.

SOLAR PLEXUS (SOLAR PLEXUS)

If the opponent is only wearing a thin shirt, this point, which is directly under the breastbone, is relatively easy to reach as it is not protected by the abdominal muscles.
A powerful punch or kick to the target area will cause the attacker to writhe in pain. However, if he is wearing a thick jacket or has strong   abdominal
muscles,   the   the probability
of being hit is very low. The short ribs are therefore usually a better target.

ELLBOGEN

A blow or a corresponding lever on the elbow joint leads to an inability to move the affected arm, up to and including a fracture.

HAND JOINT

As shown in technique 2, for example, the wrist is a painful target. It is a relatively weak joint that easily hurts and breaks when a lever is applied. As with all levers, some practice is of course required and half-heartedness when using it will inevitably lead to failure.

FINGER

The little finger is known to be the weakest part of the hand. But the other fingers are also easy to grip and can be broken if necessary.

GENITALIES

The male genitals are particularly sensitive to pain and are easy to reach with a kick, as they are relatively unprotected and located low down. The severe pain can lead to unconsciousness. Hard kicks can of course also lead to infertility.

KNIE

The knee, like all other joints, is a good target. Consistent execution is also crucial for knocking out your opponent. If you hit the knee with a kick at the right angle, you will be incapacitated. If the kick is very hard, it can also result in a nasty open leg fracture.

FOOT

The instep in particular is easy to injure with a kick. If you hit it with your heel, this will cause your opponent pain.

KICKING AND STRIKING VARIANTS

The most basic form of punching is the fist strike.
Unfortunately, you can easily injure yourself if you
don't practice and harden yourself enough (a separate
book on this topic is already in the works. However, it
is also discussed in my seminars). A hit to the chin can
be very hard, especially if the fist is not clenched
properly. You should therefore   first   the
        correct   clenching   of the   fist
correctly. The following illustrations show how it
works:

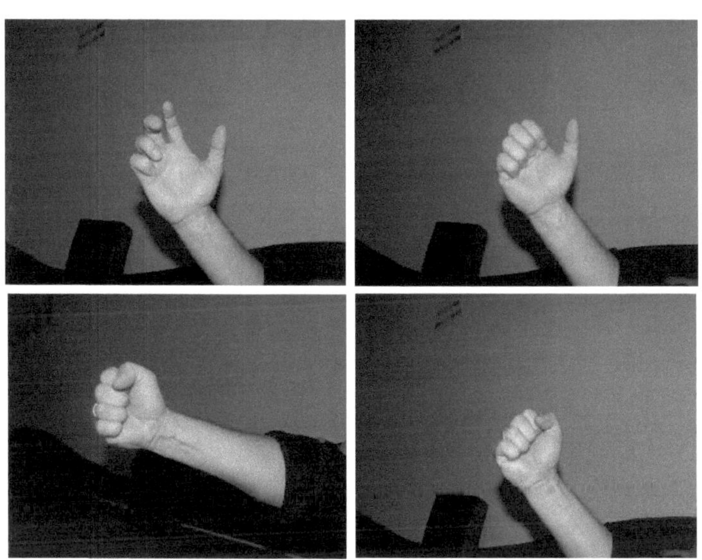

The fist kick has the best effect when you stand with your body behind the arm. You can achieve this by turning the stronger side of your body forwards. The fist only hits the knuckles of the index and middle fingers (see diagram).

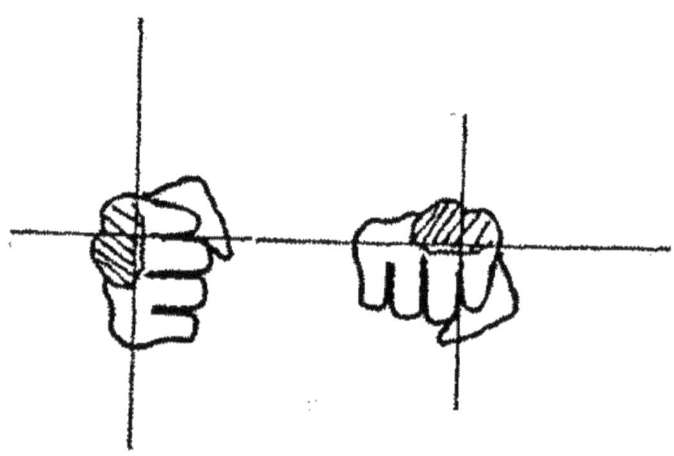

A practiced karateka rotates the fist during the punch, i.e. the inside of the fist points upwards in the initial phase of the punch and is then rotated in the course of the punch until the outside is finally on top when it hits the ground. This execution of a fist strike is quite controversial in martial arts circles, especially in kung fu. In fact, it is only advisable to strike with the knuckles shown above in order to avoid injury as far as possible.

Another striking option is the hand edge strike. A distinction is made here between the inside hand edge and the outside hand edge.

The finger thrust is particularly suitable for stabbing the eyes.

Very hard and effective techniques are the elbow strike and the palm strike to the nose.

The forward foot strike is a suitable technique for stopping an attacker. Get into the habit of not putting any weight on the front leg, i.e. your entire body weight should rest on the back leg.
This allows you to pull your leg up to the step without having to shift your weight. The kick is then delivered in two stages. Stage 1 = pull up the knee (this also provides excellent cover in case the attacker gets ahead of you). Stage 2 = the leg is pushed forward. Pull your toes far up so that the kick hits your heel. This will increase the impact and prevent you from injuring your toes.

The upward kick is also divided into two stages. However, this is not kicked horizontally, but from bottom to top. It is struck with the instep. This kick is directed towards the attacker's genitals.
The knee strike is of course part of the standard repertoire of self-defense. It can be executed from bottom to top in the genitals, as well as in the abdomen and, depending on flexibility, also in other parts of the body. A small variation is the side knee strike. This is pulled inwards from the outside. The short ribs and the outside of the thigh are good targets here.

SUMMARY

This book is not a substitute for physical training and is not the end of absorbing knowledge, but it should be enough to internalize the ideas described in it at the beginning. Always remember the technique of small steps. The more you familiarize yourself with the subject of self-defence, the more you will strive for further perfection. However, always remember that the best technique will fail if your mental attitude is not mature. Practice with a partner as often as possible. Your partner, husband or a friend will certainly support you. Also make sure that you give yourself sufficient recognition. If you are practicing with a partner, do not let them in on the technique you are about to test, otherwise they will be prepared and will not react "normally". Your opponent on the street doesn't know what to expect either. This will give you more self-confidence and security. This does not mean that your training partner should treat you like a lamb. He can really get to grips with you, but don't complain if he has to take a knock. Begin training with a moderate amount of force until you can perform the movements with some confidence. It's no shame if you don't get it right the first time. Once you have started to work intensively on self-defense, a chain reaction is triggered that can be traced back to the innate human instinct to play. However, before you go all out, you should really familiarize yourself with the individual movements.

Practice in a concentrated and constructive manner, as described in the chapter "Mental requirements". You will soon see the progress you are looking for.

Nevertheless, never forget that any attack on your person represents a great danger. Therefore, never act recklessly. Even if you have mastered a variety of techniques after a while, you will not be able to thwart every situation.
As you will have recognized, there is no fixed pattern to an attack. The external circumstances are different every time. One time it is carried out at night by an armed attacker, another time during the day by an unarmed person on a crowded streetcar. Therefore, do not lull yourself into a "false" sense of security, but only act with an overview if there is no possibility of escape. In summary, I would like to give you a few points that you should memorize indelibly, as your survival in an emergency may depend on them:

1. The best fight is the one that doesn't happen
2. If you are being held in a chokehold in any way, press your chin on the attacker's hand/forearm so that you can continue breathing.
3. If you are clutched above the arms, spread your arms outwards against the force of the opponent so that air can continue to flow into your lungs.
4. Always act with courage. Tell yourself: "He may hurt me, but I won't make it easy for him".
5. Always perform the techniques at full power. You may only have this one chance.
6. Your punches and kicks should always be delivered to the attacker's vital points.

As a member of our company, you have taken on a number of duties that require you to act conscientiously.

ask for help. If you have seriously injured an attacker, call the police or an ambulance. Even now, you are obliged to provide "first aid".
This level-headed approach will stand you in good stead in the event of a court hearing, as your act will be prosecuted (bodily injury) until it has been clearly established,
that you acted in self-defense.

END